HIGHWAY 20

Love Songs

CALIFORNIA
20

By Sam Edwards

Design by Conrad Communications, LLC (*conradcommunications.com*)

Photographs by Anders, Sam and Sita Edwards and Virginia Sharkey.

Minimal adherence to order and grammar thanks to V. Sharkey & Tom McKeown.

"The Principality of Mendocino" first published in the *Anderson Valley Advertiser*.

Eureka Productions
PO Box 660
Point Reyes Station, CA 94956

Eureka Productions
PO Box 1678
Mendocino, CA 95460

Eureka Productions
PO Box 4001
Truckee, CA 96160

Eureka Productions
92 Lafayette 3rd Floor
Brooklyn, NY 11217

www.eurekaproductions.tv
530-582-0342

Edwards, Samuel

Highway 20 Love Songs / Samuel Edwards

Manufactured in the United States of America.

ISBN-13: 978-0615710358 (Eureka Productions)

ISBN-10: 0615710352

For V.

Sutter Buttes, The Passing of Venus, June 5, 2012

A SHORTCUT THROUGH PURGATORY

I descended from the abused rock of the shoo fly complex of the Sierras
created by the old continent colliding with the ocean floor
coast bound on Highway 20
from the edge of the old continent to the new
past pillow basalt deposits at the Yuba River
where crows circled back to settle on trees extruded amid stations
bleeding the earth free of excess fluids
while the high altitude flight of geese
skewered the compass rose impeccably
not confused by the turbulence of the scavengers below;
Past the Sutter Buttes miniature volcano
visible far upwind, in the slack tide of crops and condos,
through the wetlands of gold rush gravel overflow
past the volcanic ash hoodoos of Clear Lake Oaks
listening to "Satellite of Love" left in the car
by my last ex-wife;
past Mt. Konocti with molten rock a few feet down
water and fish lumnescent with mercury –
the sunset reflected in lavic light
off the tan hue of Clearlake's waters
– clearly a shortcut through purgatory, heaven unreflected here
to the San Andreas fault at the reconsidered coast
where I might find out of geological time a place of refuge
in the Franciscan complex of the coastal range,
the extension marking the edge of the new continent's
melange of "gray wack" (muddy limestone)
that extension marking the edge of the new continent's face lift
where I'd noticed S. Groggins for sheriff-coroner
over a hand-painted Studebaker proclamation
pasted and peeling on a wall in the Colusa
of the Sacramento valley's imperative of valley value and weather.
There was Chick Montgomery's billboard
while I hurried for late Sunday service at the Ukiah Wal-Mart
no longer puzzled by the fury

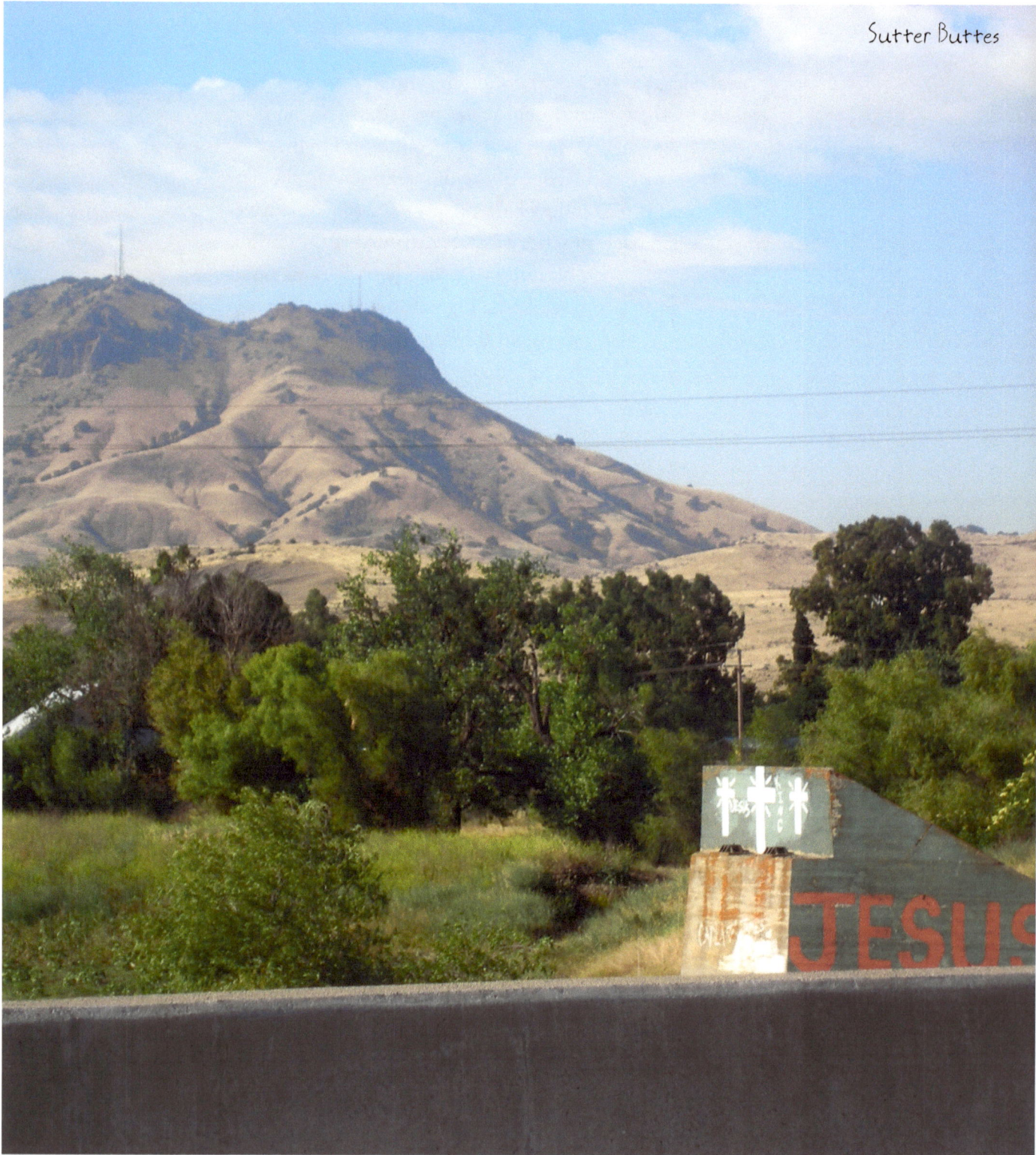

Sutter Buttes

"Past the Sutter Buttes miniature volcano visible upwind, in the slack tide of crops and condos."

of those resisting the cultural mudflow
of our slides of stuff,
hopelessly bracing the toe of descending value
– remembering Sam promises the most for the least –
hurrying on to the coast to say sorry
to an ex-wife determined
by her own genetic granite weathered
into a surviving grus, finely filigreed by life
living on the lavic exposure
oblivious of the molten undertow
of repressed discontent below.
I hurried to her
past the continuing gravel desolation of gold tailings
never stopping at official view sites bereft of view,
past an "Oasis" in foreclosure
on to the serrated edge of our ancient separation.
But there in Lake County pushing the speed limit
past roadside stands of combustible intoxicants
– no cappuccinos just yet–
newly constructed lakeside park
empty with the honesty of the pre-urban renewal reality
trying to see it all in abstraction
as an ocean current of subatomic stuff
in the equilibrium of gravity,
– learning not to see the delineation so sharply,
whether rusted Rambler or volcanic extrusion
– it's best to see peripherally
so that we can get past this time
to wind and sky and broken buildings
and abandoned cars
all here just the same.
"When you can see clearly," said my friend Willem,
"you are neither holy nor wise
just an ordinary fellow who has
completed his work."

RUMINATIONS

Just as a few days before
when visiting a son born a few minutes before his twin
in the city where the towers fell (twins to the end)
while I was viewing the hell of Ground Zero
Immense and bitterly sharp shards
erupting from the depths of fears
and underground floors of submerged consciousness
removed by fathers of fallen sons
digging for meaning
driven by memories
in an immense diabolically surviving blowhole
amongst the lesser towers
only the hoodoos of mind left there
where the working uninsured who dared to be there
— now die at a rate profit can bear —
and never allow but a little
of the grace of a sun in winter declination
while the ocean-filled winds
freeze to a heart chilling temperature
which no amount of fire retardant layers can temper
so that only a few genetically anointed
could brace to a workday in that place
acknowledged by the pre-dawn thousands
while the diligent guardians of capital's sway
filibustered any first responder give-away
waiting patiently to lighten a little
the load of uninsurable dread
while those bound fast by secondhand scripture, fearing the Buddha's
compassionate curves
compounded the shards of their feared relativity
when they fixated on a mere idea of the pure
(for they have renounced likeness)
they clutched without tenderness mundane finality.
Death is just the last word recited in a language they can't read

Foregoing the relative pleasures
of the great Satan's liberations
naturally washed onto the reefs
of affordable depravity
they played video games and ate kosher pizza
resisting Babylon's diminished evils
they unknowingly adopt the pimp's knowing sneer
they – with no internal messenger –
reached easily with similarly dulled imagination
for their true sweetheart, the Kalashnikov
or casually pushed the controls
into a final dive
exactly mirroring the sinkpool
of the weak minds they abhor.
So Al Qaeda, the Taliban and the purveyors
of cheap pleasures
grope for each other
as perhaps long separated twins
needing most of all
the mutual blow holes of Ground Zeros.

*"Learning not to see the delineation so sharply whether rusted Rambler
or volcanic extrusion. It's best to see peripherally."*

DISPATCH 3
The Fault Line of our Convictions

1.

I woke on Martin Luther King's birthday
not yet knowing what murderous sacrilege
would bring to a name day's resonance,
to a voice beside itself coming from the phone
off its cradle
the voice of someone I had thought I knew well
ranting to herself in her personal purgatory
beating back rage into a new coastline of faith
— but Tom, I keep my Walther in its belly band —
I had departed Eastern Nevada County at 7000 feet
after speaking to the other of my twins at sea level
who lives in the Apple above 125th Street
and who had thought the smoke of the Towers
to be a volcano he thought
though he couldn't bring himself to say it,
he might need some time at my latitude.
At 6000 feet I paused near the retired hanging tree

where Safeway employees now take a smoke break,
the tree sheltering a patio with benches and a historical site plaque.
Then I crested the Sierra ridge line
where I was met by a low dark squall line
that should have turned back a prudent pilot.
Instead I descended on Highway 20
the umbilical to the comfort of the Mendocino coast
and at Nevada City I turned to radio station 89.5
to be reminded of the rage still in after shock
witnessed by songs in memoriam,
(the line to our present time not yet fully developed)
across that valley scarred by gravel tailings
dredged up from under soil at least 100,000 years on the scrubbing
from primal granite,
dredged by our lust for the feel of gold,
joined by the last wedding ring I had lost,
waiting for the catastrophic flood
to restore the valley's soil for grazing and growing,
reminded by songs recorded in the field of course
that it is never too late to become a builder of dikes,
but I became distracted by the rocky debris
sluff of some ancient geologic perturbation.
– I'll thumb through my roadside rock book
at bedside for the timeline
of the soil scattered around the boulders adrift
which has only just enough nutrients for scrub oak,
growing them into insufficient stands.
I pitched into the trough of the valley,
standing muddy water barely held back by earthen dikes
-no matter no magma hardened here,
sure to be broached by the next infantile earthquake.

2.

In Afghanistan a Mujhadeen general said
the problem with the subcontinent
was of a genetic lessening by altitude
and it all drains to the plains

3.

On entering Marysville Rod Hocker asks us
to re-elect him because he's for the people.
When I passed the World of Life church
I changed radio stations there 15 miles from Meridian
where I crossed over the depths
of the Sacramento with secrets like rivers
in the southern part of America's mind
evoking a revolution
I had not dared to join.
The new program was the timeline of lynching
from the knights of the shroud of death to Cheney and friends.
And that folks is a good part of who we are now.

4.

Cardboard whipped across my view on the Sutter bypass
while to the north the Sutter buttes crumbling volcanic remains
are hidden in the mists,
as though only just now floated down
from the Trinity Alps or Mt. Lassen.

5.

But while the fields of France or Germany
are picturesque and apparently unlittered
underneath are the bones
of generation after generation of slaughter,
no worse and for sure no better
than the American eruption along the fault line of consciousness
what we did abruptly by right of divine possession.
(You know Manifest Destiny)

6.

I was actually glad to see the rise
of Lake County bulged up under low clouds.
By then from the radio: the music of a
passionate preacher's cascading vernacular

shaking the batholith of the American soul.
He said, that, voice trembling with love and fear,
all over the world and for sure here in America
profit rights had become more important
than human rights.
(The anarchists even now hesitate to say that
when driven into a dead end by New York's Finest)
And no propane stoves for Occupy Wallstreet

7.

I passed through Williams, the last of the valley towns
fenced in by rusted farm equipment,
placarded by "Retain Womble for Supervisor."
About then the soil's iron content I guess
garbled the coastal station and I heard instead
on the reflected signal the imitative conviction
of the ordinary huckster of scripture
demanding we use our worldly talents
for the glorification of the spirit of radio evangelism,
and he would ratify this upon receipt of a gift
of donations to his crusade.

8.

Climbing the grade up into Lake County's rise
I see cars on the old county road below
across the muddy wash twisting on the same vector as we
(my car, my dog and I)
cut off by our road's recent paving,
making good use of our higher inheritance of endless gravel
to a dead end in the mush oaks below
amongst which the camouflaged occupants
of predatory high sprung pick-up trucks
– I presume there must be Taliban ahead –
and I fail at first to see the faded yellow sign
"Elk crossing next five miles."

9.

Later on MLK's birthday
taking a shortcut through purgatory
I arrive at Big Oak at the east end of Clear Lake
where a confederate war flag, the stars and bars
ripped defiantly in a wind off the lake
almost lifting off in front of a small house.
A small peeling blue house desperate for repair
with an American flag in every window
and at the edge of town a pickup truck
flying another confederate stars & bars
here on Martin Luther King's Day
mounted like a Taliban 50-caliber
defiant over dual rear wheels,
past Clearlake, itself a caldera,
where what was on top
collapsed into where what was hot came from.

10.

By then I'd probably punched up Louis Armstrong
singing that he'll be glad when you're dead
you rascal you.
You messed with my wife you rascal you, he said.
But Louis has gone to the pawnshop
and got his gun you rascal you.
And I keep my Walther in its belly band.

11.

Driving into Ukiah on the way;
one end of the original dirt and gravel
thruway to Nevada City where the gold and lots of gravel came from
to find some peace by the sea
again I receive a clear signal
as MLK says across the years,
of course, we'd all like to live long lives
but we die anyway the day we deny

what we know is right.
(So now am I dead or merely waiting for the call?)
State street is lined with brand new flags
red, white and blue for the day.

12.

I arrived on the coast which is, I'm told, slipping away,
in wonder at what a seismic force MLK was,
threatening to the way we are now,
like the ocean floor in a front end collision with older Sierra rock
the way Martin was then
for his brand of non-violent confrontation
found the fault line of our convictions.

13.

But then I'm reminded that a drizzle
on the coast becomes a blizzard
when it is stopped by the significant obstructions
of the Sierras, then it is clear again
at the edge of the continent.
I notice I'd forgotten to disengage four-wheel drive
which I then do as I coast down the other side
so, too, I've forgotten to remember rage.

BIRDS-EYE VIEW OF
CLEAR LAKE *and* SURROUNDINGS
LAKE CO., CAL.

DISPATCH 4
St. Valentine's Day on Highway 20

1.

I sought marital dissolution on Valentine's Day
and I need belladonna on Highway 20 when back in the day on the way
departing from a town in the Sierra rain shadow
in the parking lot I remembered I'd lost the gift of my first wife,
a silver bracelet holding wound elephant hairs.
But there it was under my seat
held down by a tiny statue of Ganesh carved from fluerite
as I drifted down the flank of the Sierras
idling over sedimentary rock of tertiary times,
the young rocks covering rocks below of the shoo fly complex.

2.

Just before Marysville are grasslands
littered with balancing boulders of basalt.
My roadside geology book says it is "one of the nicest slabs
of old ocean floor anywhere."
I heard a newscaster there broadcasting from Cuba
or that part of Cuba which remains occupied
and where we hold prisoners without rights.
He said all things considered the cages for prisoners
weren't bad other than having to defecate in public.
He said it was regrettable but privacy was a victim
of the war on terrorism.
Didn't Captain Dreyfuss after all sleep shackled
to bed planks without the freedom to even piss?
In highway reverie I remember
my last ex putting her brother-in-law's empty 357,
in a spirit of fun,
to my head and pulling the trigger.
I probably should have heeded the warning
and I keep my Walther in its belly band.

3.

When I got to Ukiah I visited a bedbound friend
who years before thought it better I didn't come by
because of my personal conduct which so mirrored
the cold case of her own abandonment.

4.

As I wound through alluvial melange to the coast
these thoughts went around and around
as I hurried to the solace offered freely
by my second ex-wife proffering the way.
What can I say when she is still able
to offer me measured space,
for a short time at least out of mind's
desperate play.
There I am scurrying west into the sunset
of my worldly life. Via is the way.
Though I plan to stay on the road
until daylight finally breaks
I thought that back then I couldn't see
through the splattered road kill of my thoughts,
but when greeted by someone who has forgotten
to remember the aftershocks
from the magma of my petty larcenies
and has been instead actually nurtured
by the imps of time
even wearing the same earrings
given two decades before
where others change them like arcade targets.
She says with no sigh of regret
the black pearl suits her and the gold stem
causes no reaction
(remembering gold mining thrives in difficult times say I).
How do you come hat in hand
to someone not hooked on what she can't forget?
What can you do but offer the love

finally mined from some batholith
well below mind,
filled with a feeling of a tremor from the inner core,
beyond physical expectations
to a place of intimacy.
How can someone who brings you
to that place which is beyond your due,
and that's what wives and ex-wives can do
as magnetic north wanders south,
not be but another pilgrim on the way
even when it means taking a shortcut
through purgatory,
a caldera of blown out hopes –
Via is the way.
To find a place with no writ
where it seems there has always been
a perfect fit.
Perhaps the greatest thrill in a seismic search
under the watchful gaze that began it all
is bracing to the nor'wester that took us there
and whips the years like tears
from our eyes as we dead reckon
in the off-the-grid times
the true course bound for where we started.

"California 20 passes some lovely volcanic rocks in the vicinity of Clear Lake and Passes Mount Konocti, a shapely volcano still very little eroded."

Roadside Geology of Northern and Central California
David Alt
Donald Hyndman

DISPATCH 5
Serving Notice to Clear-Cutters and Crusaders

1.

Heading west on St. Patrick's Day
– my dead reckoned birthdate set back by genes and circumstance
to be an April fool instead,
I came to a stop in a spring blizzard
that I found that night on Highway 20, agitated and dark,
and giving the faintest clue of the Earth's volcanic disorder
so obvious en route by daylight.

2.

I was hurrying through the night
to have a day in a simpler perspective,
trimming an apple tree and trying to gather and remove
the fallen twigs and branches by more
than third-world happenchance.
Luckily by the end we had reinvented the one woman tie
and so we looked efficient enough to not be hooted
by power tool wielding western savants.

3.

At the communal dinner I finally saw the painting
that had hung on the wall of my house years before.
The shadowed clouds of earthen colors
parted off center by a burst of rose
like the World Trade Center in memorium sky bound lights,
reminding us of the passion of creation,
like the red rose V. repositioned on my dash
suddenly bursting in bloom overcoming me with its presence
like the red of the roadside berries there on my return,
like the red barn in the distance
centered in recently furrowed brown earth
or like red beads dangling from my rear view mirror,
flashing against the green of spring grass

Rumi says the
intelligent citizen is
not attached to where
he has been or even
to where she is but to
where they are going

And as we have learned
from Tunisia and Egypt
and environs will bear
any hardship to go
where its free

While I'm as filled
with whine as when I
followed my spiritual
teacher's lantern down
the mountain

like the red crop duster against the pale blue sky
flecked with streaks of cirrus over Sutter Buttes
even the red graffiti on an abandoned bridge footing
"Jesus."

4.

In the vernal equinox St. Patrick had foretold –
working back from the Sierra cloud barrier to where
the weather makes landfall at the source of Highway 20 –
I noticed on my arrival in a rare clear day
the fragrance of the laden air.
It should serve notice to clearcutters and crusaders
the sanctity of blooming and bonding and wild entanglements
that seem out of nowhere to appear to follow the saint's path,
so we best remember to only prune and serve
without our genetic fear of abundance
just as V. had me cut back the overgrown apple tree,
removing water shoots and ingrown twigs with no signs of life,
the tree which seemed to spread its excess for hands to tend
in anticipation of the delivery of its yield
in the intimate currency of life-giving succulence,
so that its fruit baring timeline could be extended,
and its blossoms could have freedom to germinate
among branches spread wide for the equinox dance of sun and air.
And   just as my hands have grown through the years so can the mother of
us all even in unBiblical times
increase the abundance and size of fruit to be picked.

5.

But what do humans usually do even in this rite of fertility –
but with our tacit approval –
clearcut species and people.

6.

Just before dinner V's sweater sleeve – it's ocean damp there

where the weather makes landfall – caught a delicate glass just filled.
I caught it before it tumbled from the counter,
but its stumble was enough for blood red to stream down the stem;
for pieces from the almost invisible center had disappeared.
Of course they had to be found and reconstrued.
The wine streaked down the impervious blades of knives
scabbarded between fisherman's counter and stove.
The edge of one of which I sharpened for truer cutting,
triggering me into thoughts of impermanence and illusion.
The need to be accurate in what is cut away
requires a tempered and maintained intelligence
handled with compassion.

Mount
Konocti

Clearlake

Cache Creek

Lower Lake

dam spillway

Sutter Buttes

Memorial Day

MEMORIAL DAY

I

We all bore the weight of war in the Second World war won,
now Iraq weighs not at all for the majority of us
with no citizenship papers still to accrue –
Hey! We got roots
no improvised explosive devices on the home front
where Homeland Security dollars might be
equally guarding a golf course on the Oregon coast
– earning a nice dividend for a home front warrior –
no dead leathernecks hands bound by wire
as on the cover of *Life* before MacArthur landed at Inchon
– reluctantly drawing the line at nuking past the Yalu –
Now in our times' parody of carefree days
just sales and stocks and celebrity,
and stowaways to a lost vision
– I'll just wait till it's marked down –
no helmets as tableau in boys' heart-felt beliefs,
no "loose lips sink ships" writ large above
the sailor floating on the restaurant wall
in peeling paint,
no "die hippy and find your white rabbit"
spoke by short haired dads to their sons' nodding acquaintances
no "kill them all and let God sort them out" at roadside t-shirt stands
though there were briefly "Guantanimo Country Club" bumper stickers.
Instead well earned indifference and denial hold sway
Hey! We got roots
as we flip quickly past page 4 spreads of lines at the Baghdad morgue
of bodies expertly defoliated by Makita drills in sectarian hands
clearly held by sons seemingly short of mothers' tears.
Some here, do however wonder over an espresso
– if they are among the few not wearing desert dun
who know which country has Faluga on its mind
before continuing a Sunday morning bike ride
or for those places with newspapers without front pages
to get the six packs while gassing the throaty boat for a too small lake
but six bucks a gallon will take care of that.

2

Over there they ask where have our hearts gone,
to be refugee in the limbo of box store self-interest?
"Will they ever again earn points toward the right of return?"
Can a government consume our compassion,
denying it entry at the border of our self-respect?
What more can a son say to a mother who has already foreseen
the writing on that black wall?

3

Even the Vietnam era grunt, boombox under arm,
Marine hymn at full automatic patrolling on Memorial Day
a remote coastal cemetery, full clip of red, white and blues
for each grave of someone he never knew,
knows too what it means to feel your own life in just your hands
as he rests with a sweet smile at the roots of a Monterey pine.
Even if he skipped the head of a gook who refused his request
to confess in American, low on the surface of the Mekong
and now his sleep is perhaps rarely sure (gas he says):
that too is who we drafted
then, in a sweep meant to be cost-effective

while now most of our citizens to be,
Salvadorean, Columbian, Guatamalan, Mexican
and homeboys from the Rez who can pump out on full auto with the best.
Now all waiting on their papers in desert camouflage,
playing a little rough perhaps but calling even gringos, *sir*
and throwing down with anybody
– all with a laugh –
just as would any of Whitman's riverboat citizens
waiting on territorial inclusion for citizenship
Bowie knife, K-BAR now, still stuck in a belt.
Fresh blood the draft could never sweep clean
can never sweep clean
can never ever
sweep clean
(what the hell you say
use a water cannon)
Hey! We got roots

Fight Night

At the Colusa Casino

Not taking the usual John Deere salesman cut-off Through the valley town of Colusa Where lights are out by nine And Main Street has begun the boarding up. Usual to towns without local needs.

I kept going instead on State Route 4 a couple of miles past downtown near a levee of the Sacramento River just off Highway 20's escape to the sea where on a blistering summer day it could cost a quarter for Chevron water to cool your dog.

Now like a monstrous paddle wheeler flooded from its course lying without pity in an abandoned cotton field as original people's just vengeance. There as the Colusa Casino Causeway of a surviving Pueblo Close enough to the great valley's bumper crop of condos. That no act of domestic violence should occur on fight night at the casino because most county deputies would be directing parking in the muddy stubble of hostilely harvested but thoroughly subsidized cash crops.

Though fight night was but a temporary diversion from expectant one-armed bandits. Now with digitized prosthetics waiting for busloads of chair-bound quarter players and certainly administered without mercy by corporate consultants from the gaming industry riding Crazy Horse all the way to the bank warding off Sitting Bull's ambuscade until Buffalo Bill's descendants Have scalped the last dollar from the flood tide of Sacramento's rootless evacuees from ancestral place held back by a levee of Industrialized agricultural desert increasingly broached by 1,000 acre planned communities paving over top soil first distilled by mine tailings then salted by factory monoculture so why not at least the Manifest Destiny of K.B. Homes et al so that newly required freeways can support a system of centrally planned malls linked by an exodus of real needs.

Still at the door of the casino there was pause enough for a posse of assembled scalpers of public mayhem before it was possible to enter what seemed the required industrial management of persons with plastic beer cups
- Provided to prevent uninsurable damage-
Directed down chutes to feed on video poker hnot to mention dollar machines fine tuned to the house margin.

Was there actually straw strewn for footing or was it specifically designed inside-outside carpeting of suitable design.

County deputies inside at the venue box office checked for weapons and correctly dated tickets. Inside too were the tattooed camp followers of the Generation Kill invasion force perhaps too smart to volunteer but more than able to levitate To America the Beautiful.

Certainly t-shirts and embroidered jackets conveyed some interest in pugilistic endeavors. Where banquets and bingo were more usual. Was now a raised stage With a fence and a gate in fact a cage surrounded by folding chairs.

An announcer, perhaps moonlighting from the black jack table announced that in no holds barred cage fighting. There were a few rules unlike two rule fighting where the first rule is there are no rules and the second is you can't change the first.

There was a lot of noise from boisterous greetings amongst the first couple of rows of stacked up familiars and huggers my friend Santiago, aka Saints, was to be in the tenth or eleventh bout and he waited quietly backstage in a large tent set up as the dressing room, a propane heater sucking out unnecessary oxygen.

He sat in the calm demeanor of the Shoshone warrior he is, long hair in braids for hygiene and etiquette, as though there merely to cook.

The announcer, though, had other fish to fry and by the time he remembered the issue at hand the somewhat thick mini-skirted fight night placard girls had signaled the first fight in time to be chorused by "Kill the fucker! Take him down!"

Down is where quickly one of the opposing pair found himself to be beaten into submission by the dominant fighter so that most fights were over in a couple of minutes; Plenty of time left for gaming.

Wearing what look like thick work gloves with no fingers The hurt is real enough

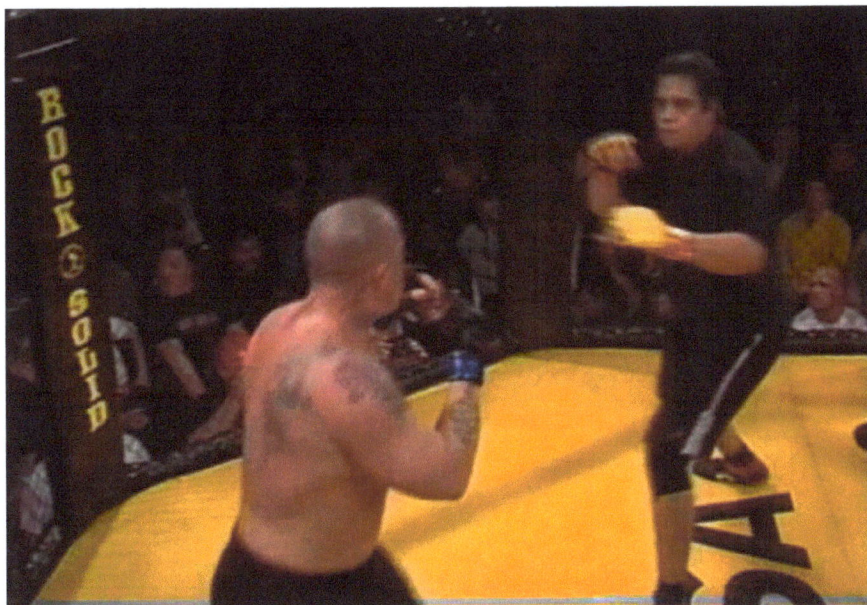

But without the safeguards of Padded boxing gloves to lengthen the fun there was blood but probably Not the brain damage of regulated competitive blood lust.

If I could have been privy to breath I suspect most were held while waiting for the gate to close behind.

Of course there was a purse - A few hundred can seem a lot when you're Behind in your rent in Yuba City or Williams.

Our man Saints entered the ring with the same smile he has for a Saturday workout with friends. Not having to hop himself up into rage, shades of Abu Grab. Entirely large but without any postures Clearly at last the natural warrior.

Saints ambled into the cage, was introduced, received the impact of his opponent's powerful charge, went relaxed to the ground as on any Saturday, letting his opponent in the mount position exhaust himself in his need to render real damage. What can be marginally understood in words. Is that he was on the bottom receiving blows with criminal intent behind them though in a relaxation impossible to fathom.

Where does that letting go spring from

if not his genetic structure allowing fingers casually bent back to forearm and able to absorb blows like cotton. Has it come to a generation not afraid of the old ways just as Anaku rode the too tall waves for his father so founding fathers risk it all for those to come.

If you know we are at bottom but light - let the suffering end and the waiting begin. That's what Saint's grandmother said to him. And as those who do the time know, "Don't cry to me, it won't help." And for sure Saints only now has a clue of that which is so true but what can you do so long As on the court spirit flows through.

He absorbed the force clearly into the circle of his forefathers so that when he finally hooked his buffed out opponent with one leg in the half guard and then flipped him just so that now his blows rained down - How though were they so much heavier? - Were Crazy Horse and Sitting Bull lending support from off this stage Or is ego the founding father of pain Why did his opponent, seemingly bred for this task alone and without the burden of a people's memory - Why did he tap out after half the number of blows, none intended to kill, and no chorus of "Hurt the fucker!"

Why?

DISPATCH 6
Likening Jesus to an Apple Tree

1.

Palm Sunday former nuns living right now down there
in the little Albion house below V. –
who came it seems as a lot more than tenants,
pilgrims at the very least who told Via she marked the way
as they bundled offerings of apple twigs,
making us know the medieval hymn
likening Jesus to an apple tree.
This old tree was covered with green shoots;
the tree people on the phone advised no radical cuts
with the tree's cycle of energy flowing up.

2.

Candelaria and Margaret's simplicity loosens the hold
of childhood proscription as they beg to garden
just as prophesied
while V. seems driven to finish this special place
while I at least seem to have entered as the donkey
for hauling and digging without fear of thought,
for I had carried garden Buddha as co-pilot
riding shotgun as we raced through Marysville and Yuba City.

3.

I had followed the signs saying spiritual retreat
pointing I'm afraid down the seldom used road
to the Seventh Day Adventist ocean research station.
But Candle and Margaret seem to know what is sanctified.
And they seem to think this small place is that
as V. transplants the roses to the front yard.
But V. knows all the parables of waiting
and preparing for what the heart needs
as she says in a poem she years ago had thought
"Silly of me," she said:

Silly of Me

I would have stayed with you forever.
I thought the golden rye grass
bowed grey to a soggy mat in winter
then rained green
was the way we'd be;
the deer at edges shy.
I thought the dark silhouette of oak-bundled hills
were our shadows embracing the valley
and the valley a velvet
hammock for our tousled limbs.
Blue knocked about tall all over the summer skies.
The black oaks grew and never hesitated.
That's why I thought when I said yes
you were looking for a place to die
and knew I was that meadow.
– V. Sharkey

Under the tangle of blackberry vines
we found our own small archaeological wonder
– A mortised stone ledge perfect for garden Buddha

DISPATCH 7
Robinson Rancheria Blues

On a summer day I was in wonder
at the proportions,
beautiful really – statuesque you might say –
of the smoke plume
rising thousands of feet concentrically in
condensed dark brown spirals while maintaining an elegant narrow waist
through which the low flying borate bombers pierced,
a single pilot only at the controls plunging into the violent updrafts,
almost being pulled apart by a tornado –
really a piñata of death gifts,
shaking as to dismember in its passion
near Reclamation Road and Highway 20
across from the throngs entering Pomo Way
to Robinson Rancheria's weekend of fun –
Damn, no one even looked up! –
concentrated on the gaming present
outsourced to those whose presence
indicated the markers of industrialized gambling,
looting the soil of memory of the roadside marker
across the newly widened highway
of the Bloody Island retribution and slaughter
for the island Indian village's
"Unjustified insurrection"
that arose from
justified exploitation where Clear Lake was
now land filled for
gringo reclamation and practical mechanized farming.
Here Buffalo Bill's
descendants will scalp the last dollar
from the flood tide of Sacramento's
rootless evacuees from
ancestral place held back
by a levee of factory monoculture

increasingly broached by 1,000-acre planned communities
paving over top soil, first
distilled by mine tailings, later
salted by industrial farming.
Perhaps my Shoshone Friend, Santiago –
Saints for short –
will fight here for a month's rent
in a temporary cage
amid the slots, beer in plastic cups only, no glass allowed.
He did so already in the
Colusa Casino just past the cut-off favored
by John Deere salesmen navigating the tributary
of Highway 20 bisecting
the Great Valley with the promise of riches.
Foundered mine tailings then, up to the vast fields of condos now .
Saints long braided hair
framing movement as relaxed as throwing down on a Saturday ,
and his uncle in his corner added
"Those who do the time know
Don't cry to me it won't help / let all this shit wash away
I'm not going anywhere I tell them
It's just as much as before – still mine."

Sutter Buttes

DISPATCH 8 - TAKE 2

1.

(Easter news was of the Church of the Nativity occupied and surrounded)
Rather than mourning for the first time on an Easter morning
we pilgrimaged a little to honor the day,
finding that joining others with open hearts is the way,
the service on the peak of the mountain
noting Torrey Pine in barest cracks truncated
by wind and circumstance — was picked at seeming random
when with my kids I joined those gathered
very untypically for me with tears filling my eyes.
The scripture from Hildegard was of renewal,
decrying in song the fragile halo of moisture
surrounding the planet awaiting to germinate,
and bring life like the shoots on the old apple tree.
Experiencing Christ risen was a natival thing
as our intrinsic resonating selves
beyond mere meat certainly not that bull in a China shop
and then my littlest said knowing I'd forgotten

that he had painted four eggs exactly enough for us.
As my birthday was April Fool's Day the next day,
my kids gave me a pocket watch with pendulum its innate message –
that rhythm will always triumph over sequential time –
as the hands stopped at quarter to an hour passed.

2.

So I headed down the hill racing west
where I've found time is malleable and restorative,
Bessy Smith singing out her own heartbeat best
germinating across the years.
But as I pedaled to the metal going nowhere fast,
I realized that with intention time stays immovable
or restarts to a geologic clock
that in fact I would have to surrender
for time to enshroud and enfold and comfort.
So that finally when I let the road run
I arrived at the ocean,
prepared for plans to be amiss
but on the local store's bulletin board studded with rusty staples
was the very announcement of my intentions to remain
from twenty years before.
And when the sisters of the Assumption opened their door
there to release a moth
and it gave a man's resonance to their names
with barely a flinch Candle and Margaret greeted me
arms spread wide with a supper still improbably in the single ladle,
of leeks and potatoes, the soup of the poor
embellished by companionship and worship.
And by adding that still mysterious water to the wine
there with the chunk of cheese, heel of bread
a feast to go with the talk of the sacred
in the small unnoticed things like the few sips divine,
not needing carefully calculated introduction.
The Assumption sisters soothed me when I expressed my troubles,
believe in Him or not they said

but give the devil his due.
It's been going on since the civic discord in heaven.
And of course I asked –
about how much meaning there is in ancient culture
– Candle's family have lived in the same house for a thousand years –
when the butchers are born equally
among relics and bulldozed memories?
But these Sisters urged me to read Merton who struggled
finally succumbing to the lightning bolts
symbol of the age of electrocution.
In Thomas' case by bath
as the Romans liked the highway symmetry
of the precisely aligned crucified.
But Candle and Margaret see small signs of awakening
of consciousness, even some awareness, of the needy
they showed me the Palm Sunday apple twigs now flowered,

DISPATCH 9
I Will Marry You and I will Bury You

I waited patiently for a sighting at the Nevada county seat
just after the Friar Tuck fire in the old town
just off Highway 20 listening to some charged lyrics
"I will marry you and I will bury you,"
(actually a very romantic line)
although there was an ATF bomb investigation truck parked ahead.
Just then Carmelo ambled around the corner from 18 years before
noting that without rose colored glasses
the world would be a slightly sadder place
which reminded me of the giant statue of Buddha
which the Taliban had without mirth mined, torpedoed and pulled down.
But my living Buddhist loan shark tells me to stay rooted.
She gave me for instance with a hand shake the means to remain
and at altitude to boot, though driving to the sea sets me free.
And the stories from there unlike those of me
are of men and women going against the tide.
Even in a reprint in the Beacon of the stay of a hundred years before
a steel steamer with a load of paving
brought off the Ukiah throughway broaching off Albion, its load
bound for mansions to be rebuilt in the scorched and rubbled meadows
of Babylon by the Bay
to ensure the psalms remain true to the life of rescue,
without monuments or quotation away from family content.
And this too the date the Titanic foundered
while the California steamed away with its radio operator asleep.
Perhaps that is why my teachers say don't be lazy,
know they say the stars are in procession
and the axis of the Earth wobbles every 26,000 years.
Just as in spinning a beer can
we'll find Orion's Belt was there before
to see the offset of the Pharoah's tombs

"Over a million feet of lumber (was) shipped from the new wharf at Greenwood Landing last month in addition to large amounts of ties, etc."

Mendocino Beacon
April 10, 1886

foretelling perhaps that Lincoln would be shot this day
And Whitman would sing, "Oh Captain, oh Captain,
my Captain, it's some dream
You've fallen on the deck cold and dead."
So then finally is this feeling I have of resurrection?
Are the pilgrim ladies right and this is the time
like the vine enveloping the acacia tree we later trimmed?

THE PRINCIPALITY OF MENDOCINO

Blacksmithing STILL ALIVE

Mendocino County's Public Radio transmits the Near and Far, the Left and Right, Up and Down of what in a pretty red state seems a principality, an enclave, a refuge, the Principality of Mendocino.. The somewhat eccentric electronic emissions encircling the principality start before state route 128 hews up the valley from Boontling times to the champagne ways of some of these days.

But when I arrive late at night in the township, the village seat, the center of Gravity of Mendocino proper, the only apparent emissions are from the Mendocino Art Center studios. That, and of course Paterson's Pub and Dick's Bar, keeping it from small town, not even late night, shut down.

Besides a little light pollution and the rebound from a westerly surf one hears the sometime clang bang of hammers on blacksmith anvils in the open shed space of the foundry. A glow marks the spot from the forges rewelded by the current master smith and probably just a few minutes ago thought by some " as not suitable for the center's mission."

When before Mendo proper I approached the oldest wooden highway bridge in California – way above the Albion flat – I scurryed across while it was still standing, leaving central Albion behind. All of which gave me flashback of the smudged black and white photos of early Coastal mill life which was a lot like Siberian industrial days – let the nostalgia go! The tourist packs will come anyway.

But Doug's Albion store looking its 1950's way still like the photo of the wood paneled Chevy station wagon being pumped gas at an impossibly low price – way below two bits – by the granddad of someone 'farming' a little up the ridge in Albion Nation.

The back of Doug's building always will house the Volunteers' pumper truck as well as the too frequently needed jaws-of-life kinds of tools for coastal highway speeders. Throughout this Rhode Island – sized county, volunteer groups like these sustain the heart beat of the place the corporations cut and ran from. And the various volunteers are reinvigorated by newcomers determined to finally stay put, no matter how much moisture their laundry wicks in. And then, after skirting the moonlight's shore bound sheen, and seen between the several fishing trawlers anchored in Little River Cove, the memory of single lunged packet boats moored precipitously to load timber for San Francisco's rebirth after the Great Quake in redwood clear enough to reveal your better self.

While in the pitch and heave off Portagee Beach near the mouth of Big River, loading board– feet on sliding decks in sudden lurching swells initiated from some remote underwater mountain range, that sometimes mangled hands and feet ready for the compassionate knife of Mendocino's Dr. Preston who again, on occasion, was to be covered in gore like his days just after the Great Quake. "Only better than Civil War field hospitals in that we had something for the pain."

Or it might have been a timberman struck blind in the craftsman eye by a glint of steel off a band saw or his skeleton compacted after a topper's fall. But remembrance of the heft and feel of those days is not in selective remnants of the past we've chosen to forget: no picturesque buildings well maintained of the missing towns (Glen Bair, Dewey, Melbourne, Christine) They had hotels and cafes and blacksmith shops, stables, saloons and narrow gauge rail yards. Now only foundation debris.

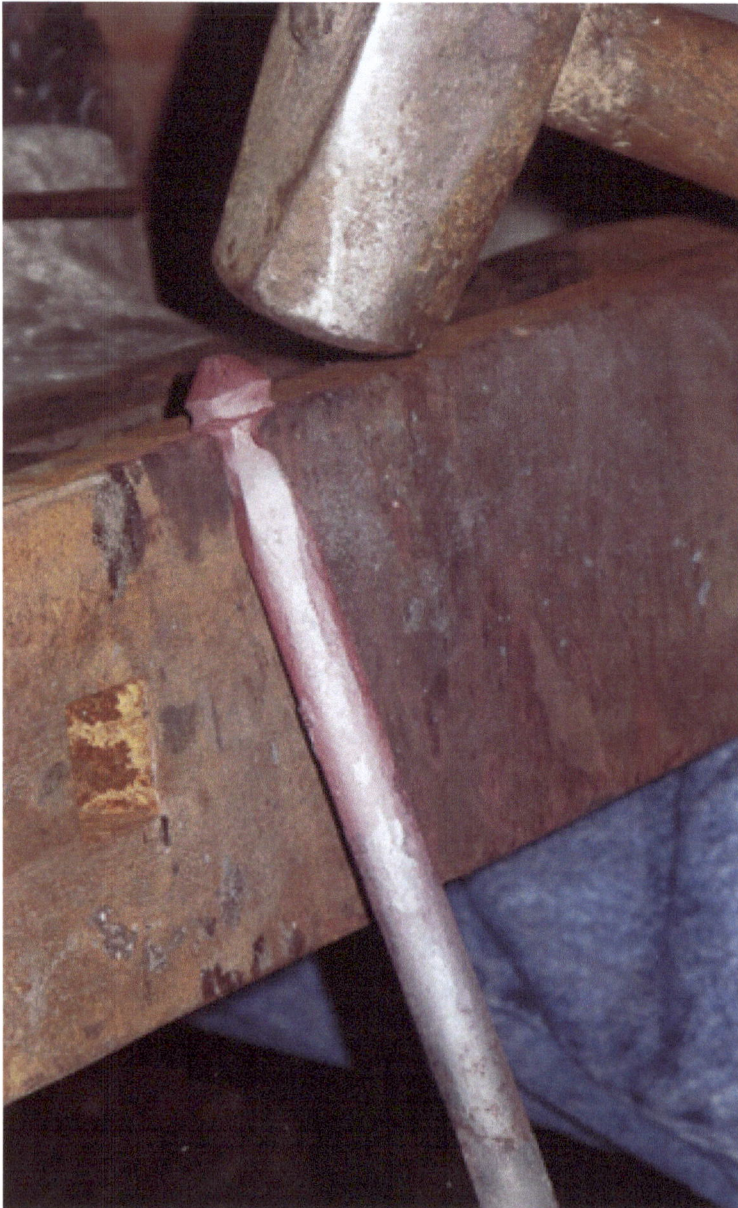

And then there were the countless port towns at every cove and eddy [Cuffey's Cove, Whitesboro, Big Gulch, Bridgeport, Nip and Tuck, Hardscratch, Kibesillah, Laguna, Pallas Bay.

These served that wild north coast ocean highway which brought the first automobiles here by ship when Mendo's many rivers and deep gully creeks finally had bridges to parallel the timbered logging train bridges which served the camps at every cove and landing.

No jetties survive to serve nostalgia's trade, Pt. Arena not withstanding, (remember it really was not so picturesque). Hardly a board is left of any of this (recycled I guess): no buildings, no markers, no plaques, no tourist vistas of boom to bust days. Merely on occasion, an overgrown cemetery, or stapled photos outside a few stores and tourist picture book memorabilia and then of course the tidied up exception of the entire historical review board approved Mendocino township.

Oddly enough this trade in, and often enough exploitation of, nature's free trade still has hands- on descendants of the original trades. The forges dampened roar of opened doors in the midst of Mendo's high class touristville is music to what is still molten in the heart of this crazy, mismatched marriage of a place. A place where third generation and late bloomers and tardy arrivals are in a creative dynamic.

No death and potatoes of a world already mourned and past, and no succumbing to well oiled New-Age carpet baggers (well maybe a little) putting plastic over their sweat lodges. The Art Center for instance in its well used habitat – some would say rundown ways – is a living testimony, a poetic memory, maybe a creative reconstruction of this county's white man's frontier days, "What Indians? Find me a buck who will take down a fifteen foot across redwood giant!"

It may not seem important to boards of directors, but the funky old forges in the back sheds connect directly to the old ways, with tools of a bygone time often enough shaped and pounded ("only when hot enough") from the debris field of those days: giant cast couplings and joints from fourth generation backyards, or venturing afield, to Ukiah auto dismantlers, steel parts on the cheap with a high carbon content or auto springs suitable for the tests of ancient craft's current practitioners.

For as Ernie Pardini famously said "As long as one gypo remains (meaning in this case one independent non-corporate logger) we're all free."

Thank God for the ear blasting scream of the volunteers base station sirens!

EPILOGUE

Sutter Buttes appear to be a seismic afterthought
when you first notice them
which when you are on an old ocean floor
are impossible not to see
but they gain in importance
with the harvesting
and planting of rice and strawberries.
Despite yourself you progress to a sense of place.
I think it was Memorial weekend
that I raced to Lakeport
halfway to the coast
to sleep on the fishing dock
trying to balance positive and negative.
Andre said he found the inner breath
that essential place in between
while diving in fluorescent water
and a friend of Frank's
while in an asthmatic attack
which then in wonder he would trigger
as in need he might.
And I merely while weeping
foresaken but not bereft.
That's where I found my breath
extolled for thousands of years
as the heart center becoming the starting place
for thought and action,
that crater formed by collision
with sun energy as the first teacher
embraced by Earth's pulsing vortex.
Then finally with persistence
the body achieves central equilibrium
as that equinox within respiration
does the conscious work.
Probably and profusely a little late for me

as my shell of flesh tries to implode
breath shaking itself free
just as the old continent
smashed into the ocean floor
marked by the standing wave of the Sierras.
And briefly I had a serenity
as that cloaking a semi
loaded with crushed cars
pulled off Highway 20 by Williams
cab saturated in the truth of a sunset.
Then under the relief of the single tree
in Frank's Ukiah backyard
we faced apart,
hand to the other's heart
before the primal intrusion of grappling
in a pleasure similar to an Afghan greeting
"Salaam Aleikum."
This while V. at the Mendocino lighthouse
was being swooped by a hawk
not appreciating tourism.
She with grey lifting surfaces
actually brown and white V. told me later.
Pretty clearly from the report
a marsh hawk
while in the cove the affirmation
of harbor seals below
in eye contact before deep water acrobatics
which the keeper offhandedly reported
was the same for all to see
and receive that benediction
not yet available there by shuttle bus.
I waited in Albion for Vince and V,
who had paddled around the bend
out of black and white
and where I would have expected
tangled grey and damp

they reported Technicolor beyond fog line
perhaps from V.'s insistence
not unlike inner breath's persistence.
Maybe my teacher is right
and the Ganges depicts the pilgrimage
in a body made awake by conscious respiration
which is all it takes
for the end of dissatisfaction
— who knows maybe even deforestation —
for I've seen Afghans in a terrain similar
to that passed by the Denver train
of the depressed backyards of Helper, Utah
but with acceptance and hugs
which Vince said came easy for Italians too,
and V. said that's what men's groups perhaps learned
and I said in that case
a bow would be truer.
Warriors and firemen learn to hug
but in an intimacy thoughtfully shared
for me having witnessed returned Afghans
kiss the ground
I'm forced to consider
that all who come home should too.

THE BLOODY ISLAND MASSACRE
And Going Native to Protect Truly Private Property

"If you're a First Nations tribe in Lake County, California, United States of America, you can provide 100 painstaking pages proving under the federal government's own property laws that you own a piece of land, and the Board of Supervisors still vote against you on grounds of 'protecting private property.'

"It happened on September 6, 2011 in Lakeport – a date that will live in infamy in the oft-bloody annals of regional aboriginal-settler relations.

"The land at issue is an island known traditionally as Elem Modun, now commonly referred to as Rattlesnake Island: the cultural and spiritual center of the Elem Pomo, who have lived in and around southeastern Clear Lake for at least 10,000 years. For 6,000 years of those years, if not far longer, **Rattlesnake Island has been a burial grounds, site of several villages, and ceremonial area for Elem. Archeologists have dated artifacts on the island to 14,000 years old, some of the earliest documented evidence of human occupation in the western hemisphere.**

"Both the 56-acre island and the 50-acre Elem reservation lie slightly southeast of that now-stagnant, once thriving former resort town along the Highway 20 corridor, Clearlake Oaks. As I described in

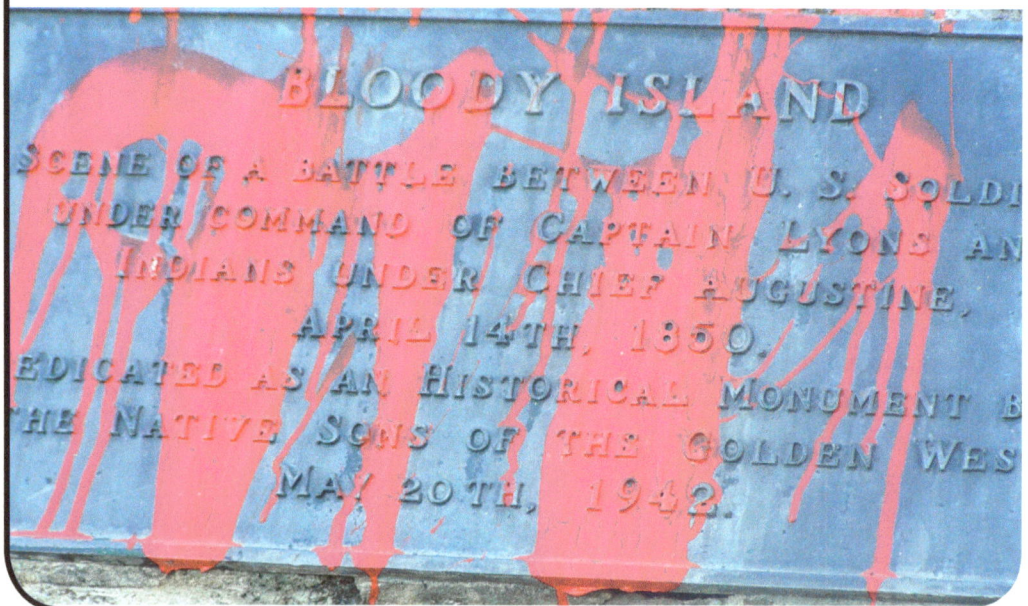

BLOODY ISLAND
SCENE OF A BATTLE BETWEEN U. S. SOLDI
UNDER COMMAND OF CAPTAIN LYONS AN
INDIANS UNDER CHIEF AUGUSTINE,
APRIL 14TH, 1850.
DEDICATED AS AN HISTORICAL MONUMENT B
THE NATIVE SONS OF THE GOLDEN WES
MAY 20TH, 1942.

a piece for the Anderson Valley Advertiser entitled 'The Struggle for Rattlesnake Island,' the island was essentially stolen in 1877....

"A familiar pattern had emerged among those supporting Nady, (who is the current developer claiming ownership-ed.) who seemed more interested in discrediting the significance of the Elem's prior occupancy of their land than in actually weighing in on the subjects immediately at hand. If a supervisor asserted that their own family has lived for a long time in Lake County, and that this longevity is equivalent to being "native" to the area, you knew they were about to vote in favor of granting Nady's appeal.

"As he prepared to cast the deciding vote, Board Chairman Jim Comstock started out thusly: 'My family's been living in Lake County for 150 years. You can't get more native than that!"
—Will Parrish
Anderson Valley Advertiser
September 21, 2011

"One of the largest such massacres took place in 1843, when a Spanish military expedition under the command of Salvador Vallejo burned approximately 200 Pomo villagers alive inside their traiditional roundhouse on Indian Island in Clear Lake, located on Koi Pomo territory. The natives' crime was that they refused to submit to slavery at Salvador Vallejo's 66,000-acre rancho, a parcel that spanned much of Sonoma, Napa, and Lake counties.

"From May 15-17, 1850, the US Army carried out what is today known as the Bloody Island massacre. After a group of Pomo men retaliated for years of murder and rape by settlers Andrew Kelsey and Charles Stone (the town of Kelseyville is named after the former), the US Army responded by slaughtering roughly 60 Pomos near Kelsey's ranch, followed by the arbitrary slaughter of 75 Pomo far away from where the incident took place, along the Russian River."
—Will Parrish
Anderson Valley Advertiser
August 24, 2011

☞ For more information concerning the campaign to return Rattlesnake Island to the Elem, visit *www.elemmodun.org*.

www.ingramcontent.com/pod-product-compliance
Lightning Source LLC
Chambersburg PA
CBHW041545040426
42447CB00002B/48